FISHING THE WORLD

FISHING THE WORLD

CATCHING THEM ALL!

Steen Ulnits

authorHOUSE®

AuthorHouse™
1663 Liberty Drive
Bloomington, IN 47403
www.authorhouse.com
Phone: 1-800-839-8640

E-mail: steen@ulnits.dk
Website: www.ulnits.dk

First published by AuthorHouse   09/23/2011

ISBN: 978-1-4670-3370-1 (sc)
ISBN: 978-1-4670-3369-5 (ebk)

Printed in the United States of America

This book is printed on acid-free paper.

CONTENTS

PREFACE

I have been very fortunate indeed. I have been able to turn my passion for fish and fishing into a profession—in many ways. First, as a fishing tourist, then as a fishing guide, then as a fisheries biologist and finally as a fishing writer and photographer.

This has taken me to exotic parts of the world where exotic fish species await in exotic surroundings. Paradise for any angler, young and old. But especially so for a fisherman who is also a biologist. For me, the real challenge has always been to visit, see and catch indigenous species in their natural habitat. That was always my mission. Visiting native waters, experiencing the surroundings and then hooking up with their finned inhabitants is what really makes me tick.

In this book I have compiled a list of some 60 fish species that I have encountered and caught on my trips to way over 50 countries since my first trip abroad as a young student in 1974. They represent the majority of popular game fish species found around the globe. But it is in no way a complete list as there never will be one. Bony fishes comprise more than 30.000 clearly defined species, plus a good number of species yet to be identified!

I hope that you will enjoy travelling with me—be it on your mobile phone, tablet, laptop or desktop Mac or PC. This book can be read on all of the above devices!

Steen Ulnits

SPECIES ON MY LIST

It takes a lot of work and preparation before you are ready to do battle with exotic species in far away countries. You have to know as much as possible about your quarry—about its biology, fishing seasons, suitable tackle etc. Otherwise you will end up as I have done myself several times—in the perfectly right place at the perfectly wrong time . . .

The first time I experienced this was deep in the Amazon, in the border region between Venezuela and Columbia. Weather was great, surroundings impeccable and lodgings fantastic—but the Amazon River itself almost 12 metres too high for fishing . . . The end result was one week of fruitless fishing amongst the highest tree tops—with not a single peacock bass caught.

Fortunately, you learn from your experiences, and incidents like this become the exception to the rule. And these days, if you are a wealthy person, you can easily buy your way out of troubles like these. You simply book a cabin, a boat and a guide from one of the many renowned fishing lodges in the area that you want to visit. Tell them what you want to catch and how—and they will tell you exactly when to come. They will also tell you exactly what to pay before going . . .

Since I was never a wealthy person, I have had to carve my way to the best fishing spending a lot of time researching and asking questions. This is a time consuming process but has the added bonus of getting you in touch with several local anglers willing to share their knowledge. I am deeply thankful to all of them, many having become close friends over the years.

When I first visited Greenland in 1974 I was but 18 years. The world was big and the internet had not yet been invented. Thus it was way more complicated than it is today to gather the information necessary before going fishing in far away places. But it was also much more of an adventure than it is today. Today, you can get to even the most remote areas of the world in one or two days.

The world has shrunk rapidly, and fishing has deteriorated at an alarming rate. I am grateful to have visited some fantastic areas in time and experienced some outstanding fishing that may not be there in the future. If we don't take the necessary measures to protect it. If we don't enlarge existing nature preserves and set up new sanctuaries.

When in Alaska for the first time in 1976, the Iliamna area offered but four fishing lodges. Today, the air is full of buzzing float planes and helicopters during the hectic summer months. Thus the "wilderness" here has become a lot tamer than it was in 1976 . . .

Still, this world offers some great fishing to be experienced by modern anglers. And I still have species on my list that I have to meet and do battle with. But never forget the fight against the ever increasing pressure on remaining natural resources. They won't be there forever if you don't protect them against being exploited by greedy human beings like you and me . . .

Well, time for you to meet some of the fish that I have met over the years!

ARAPAIMA—
PERU

The Amazon River Basin of South America is home to one of the largest freshwater fishes of the world—the mighty arapaima.

It is a lung breathing bony fish that may reach weights of 200 kgs. It has delicious white meat which has made it attractive to local indians as well as colonizing Europeans for centuries. Especially the Portuguese fell in love with the arapaima as its white flesh reminded them of their beloved cod back in Europe. A sad fact that has also put this magnificent fish on the list of endangered species . . .

As a lung breathing fish the arapaima spends most of it time and life in shallow water near the surface. In the breeding season arapaimas show themselves a lot, splashing around and occasionally even jumping clear out of the water, making them vulnerable to spear fishing.

In most places it is now prohibited to catch, eat and sell arapaima so maybe and hopefully this great species will be preserved for the future. Unfortunately, the use of invisible monofilament nets has not yet been prohibited. Thousands of protected and illegal arapaima are caught in these nets every year . . .

Apart from its delicious meat, the giant bony scales of the arapaima are used for decorative purposes. Also, parts of its oral bones are used by the locals as very efficient sandpaper!

This particular arapaima took a rattling plug and was quickly released to spawn again. Our native guide was very careful to regularly pour water over its coarse gills while we were unhooking it and taking pictures. To prevent them from drying out in the Amazon heat.

It was great to see a native Indian take such great care of his local treasures. He really cared. And so should we.

Arapaima—Amazon River—Peru

ARCTIC CHAR— GREENLAND

I 1974—18 years old—I was on my first trip to Greenland. The fishing wasn't as fantastic as it can be up there but Mother Nature more than made up for it in other ways.

This young fisherman was completely taken with the majestic drifting turquoise icebergs, the blowing humpback whales, the waving northern lights, the pretty Eskimo girls and everything else up there. It was the first visit out of countless later trips. Seriously, I have no idea whatsoever how many times I have been to Greenland since 1974. As a simple tourist. As a serious photographer. Or as a hard working fishing guide.

I 1985 I even spent all of July, August and September up there—fishing, boating, trekking and hunting caribou to finish off the season as the first snow started to fall. My then parents in law lived up there and so I had easy access to a big boat that could take me to all the best places. What a privilege.

This particular arctic char was caught spinning in a deep lake in the Nanortalik area of southern Greenland. On my very first visit to "Kallalit Nunat" as the Eskimos call it—"Land of the Humans". It took a 15 gram ABU Salar spoon and was eaten with great pleasure—and quite some hunger. It was served with delicious chilled runoff from the nearby mountains!

After dinner, whisky was served with chunks of ancient and dark blue inland ice drifting as icebergs in the fiords. Just floating around for the taking—if you could get to them, that is!

Amazing to think that this particular kind of ice which cracked audibly in the glasses, had fallen as snow on top of the massive inland ice thousands of years ago . . .

Arctic char—Taersserssuaq—Greenland

ARCTIC CHAR—
LABRADOR

Being spoilt with arctic char from Greenland, why bother to go all the way across the Davis Strait to Labrador to catch the very same species there?

Simply because arctic char grow a lot bigger here! In Greenland a 10 pound char is a giant whereas in Labrador and Quebec you may well hook a 20 pound+ fish.

Feeding in and around the rugged shoreline of Labrador simply provides char with more food than the colder waters off Greenland. Amongst the majestic drifting icebergs here food is scarcer and the feeding season shorter. This is simply the reason for Labrador and Quebec being the true hotspots (no pun intended as they are mostly freezing cold paces!) if you are looking for seriously big char.

This particular 10 pounder was caught on a small #8 Black Woolly Bugger fished dead drift between several rolling fish in a glacial lake. A few days earlier I had met a very nice 71-year old gentleman from Toledo, Ohio.

Tony was flying around in his own Beaver floatplane as he had done each summer ever since the Second World War. And since his fishing buddy had just had a heart attack, Tony was forced to go by himself. He felt like having some company so offered me the vacant passenger seat in his Beaver.

I didn't hesitate to accept his generous offer and spent two wonderful weeks with him fishing one completely untouched water after the other for brook trout, arctic char and Atlantic salmon. I couldn't have been happier!

Just minutes before landing the char pictured, I was spooled by a giant fish that never showed itself. Still today I often wonder how big it was. It just took off and emptied my reel, never showing itself.

Maybe I had hooked into a stray Russian nuclear submarine, strategic Goose Bay Air Base not being far away?

I'll never know . . .

Arctic char—Clyho Lake—Labrador

ARCTIC GRAYLING—
ALASKA

Grayling are very prolific in many areas of Canada and Alaska where they inhabit slower sections of the rivers. Arctic grayling are easily distinguished from their European cousins by the presence of small teeth in the mouth (the European having none) and a larger dorsal fin. Plus some magical pink and purple rim markings on their large fins.

Overall, Arctic grayling are much more predatory than the European grayling though both feed primarily on insects and crustaceans. In Alaska it is not at all uncommon to catch large grayling on big red and white Dardevle spoons intended for pike! European grayling would never sink that deep. They are more sophisticated . . .

Arctic grayling rarely exceed 2 pounds and 20 inches but are eager surface feeders rising freely to dry flies throughout the short summer. The largest specimens are typically caught in the waters around Great Bear and Great Slave Lake in North America where 4 pounders are caught on a regular basis.

In the short summer months after ice out, that is. Ten out of twelve months have the lakes covered with thick ice preventing even the hardiest dry fly fisherman from having any action!

Arctic grayling are found in Asia as well as in North America giving this particular species a very large geographical distribution—probably the largest of all salmonoids. Only rivalled maybe by the Sibirian lenok.

Arctic grayling—Lake Kijik—Alaska

ATLANTIC MACKEREL— DENMARK

Mackerel are macknificent fish—in almost any way. Pound for pound they are the strongest fish that swim in northern waters, being miniature copies of the giant bluefin tuna which also once frequented our Scandinavian seas.

As happened with tuna, overfishing has broght stocks of mackerel on the brink of extinction but luckily, stocks have recovered in recent years. Unfortunately, the same hasn't happened with the tuna—due to continued overfishing in the Mediterranean.

Every year huge schools of hungry mackerel enter Scandinavian waters—usually in May. When the water warms, they get close to shore where they hunt sprats and herrings with such eager that some of them forget themselves, get caught by a wave and end up on the sandy beaches. Not exactly what they had in mind for breakfast . . .

These close shoreline encounters usually happen in August when warm easterly winds have allowed the waters to clear up. Mackerel have dense gill rakers, used for filtering plankton, that don't function well in murky and sandy waters. Thus the huge schools of mackerel stay out of reach when breaking waves from predominant westerly winds produce turbid water along the Jutland westcoast.

There is only one bad thing to say about this macknificent fish: Mackerel have dark and tasty meat that decays very rapidly. Going mackerel fishing in warm August weather makes no sense if you don't bring an ice box or at least a cooler for your catch . . .

Mackerel are very fatty fish so don't try to fry or steam them. They taste too much like fish prepared that way . . . No, instead they are just so good when you smoke them.

And don't be short on pepper if you choose this option!

Atlantic mackerel—Agger Tange—Denmark

ATLANTIC SALMON—
ICELAND

Most people associate Atlantic salmon with bright, silvery fish fresh from the ocean. But fact is that salmon only retain this look for a short time once they leave the feeding grounds in the ocean and ascend their rivers of birth to spawn.

Quickly they change their silvery ocean dress into something dark and more suitable. Their thin skin with its loose scales thicken and the scales become firmly embedded in the skin that turns various shades of brown. The males develop a big kype making them look very impressive indeed. The purpose being to scare other males and impress the females.—Sounds familiar, doesn't it?

Personally, I love to follow this amazing development which—when completed—has turned the same animal into something completely different. From silvery feeding machine in the ocean to fasting breeding machine in the river. One cannot help but being impressed—especially when you consider the distance that some salmon travel. We are not talking hundreds of kilometres. We are talking thousands.

From this perspective I am equally fascinated with catching the dark coloured salmon in their spawning dress. They don't run as long or leap as high as fish fresh from the ocean. But they strike hard and put up a good battle, being very determined not to leave the pool they have come to love!

This particular salmon was caught in Iceland—in late September in a beginning snow storm. That fact alone made it very memorable. It was bitterly cold . . .

Atlantic salmon—Vopnafjordur—Iceland

ATLANTIC SALMON— LABRADOR

Atlantic salmon are amazing fish. Born in freshwater rivers they migrate downstream into the salty ocean where they feed voraciously and grow both big and strong.

When they become mature they simply turn around and return to the exact spot where they were born. Quite often with impressive accuracy. Obviously they are born with state of the art GPS devices built right in! Programmed with the right coordinates too . . .

Well, I followed this returning Atlantic salmon back to its place of birth in the upper Eagle River, Labrador. We had to fly in by float plane and then access the river in canoes. Quite a strenuous affair but it had the obvious benefit of getting rid of all competing fishermen! We didn't see a single salmon fisherman on "our" pools all week!

In the Upper Eagle River all salmon have lost their silvery coat from the ocean and put on their colored spawning dress. Still they are quite a match on a light single handed fly rod.

This 12 pounder took a #4 Cossebom and was quickly returned to spawn. It was the last fish of a very memorable evening which started out with two grilse caught in very shallow water while sitting on a shoreline rock making short casts into the current. It doesn't have to be complicated!

Later, when I waded into the pool and started casting, my green fly was immediately engulfed by eager brook trout in the two to four pound range. In fact I managed 10 brookies in 12 consecutive casts—as witnessed by my friendly Eskimo guide. Fishing was crazy.

Then I waded in as deep as I dared, cast a long line across the strong current, mended once—and hooked this magnificent salmon. What a way to finish off a fantastic day's fishing!

Atlantic salmon—Eagle River—Labrador

ATLANTIC SALMON— NORWAY

In the Long Run it pays to persevere—to search the water and fish the Long Hours. In the Long Run you may hook the fish of a lifetime—or no fish at all.

This particular Atlantic salmon was caught in the Long Run—litterally! It took my #4 Green Highlander double in a beautiful pool named "Long Pool". The saying goes that it was named after its length but I suspect there might be another even more plausible explanation, namely the Long One:

To get to Long Pool you need to take a Long Walk. But that alone won't get you there. You also have to climb a Long Railway and walk on top of it for a Long Distance. On one side there is a steep mountain slope—on the other there is a deep drop down into the gorge. A Long Way down . . .

And at any time you might be caught off track (!) by the train going by. The only way out then is to jump into the bushes and hope for the best!

Imagine what it felt like walking the railway carrying this freshly caught 20 lbs. salmon? Well, it certainly felt like a Long Way and I certainly got Long Arms! The fish just grew heavier with each step. Fortunately, the Long Train never materialized.

Anyway, fishing Long Pool is always worth the Long Walk. A Long Fight might well be awaiting you there . . .

And back at the lodge in the evening, sitting comfortably in front of the crackling fireplace, it doesn't have be a Long Time between drinks . . .

Time to celebrate, well into the Long Hours!
Longing for Norway as I write this . . .

Atlantic salmon—Gaula River—Norway

BARRACUDA—
FLORIDA

Barracuda are widely overlooked as game fish—for some weird reason. Fact is that nothing much compares to the blitz-like strike of a big barracuda. When it spots your fly, you will not be able to see the actual strike. All of a sudden it just has that fly of yours in its mouth!

And things don't slow down after that. Barracudas are some of the very few fish that can actually outswim a bonefish and eat it. Runs will be blistering and there is just no stopping a big 20 pound+ barracuda when it wants to leave your flat and heads for the open ocean . . .

For all these good reasons, more and more flyfishermen target barracuda specifically. It certainly provides the stuff for memories of a lifetime—perfectly on par with traditional gamefish like bonefish and tarpon.

Maybe the majority of fly-caught barracudas are caught on very long needlefish patterns in fluorescent green and orange colors—trolled at high speed after a moving boat. This makes for some very memorable strikes but it isn't sight fishing which is always the most fun and the most demanding.

This particular specimen took a bright green popper cast close to the shoreline near the beautiful Marquesas off Key West. On its first run it took way over a hundred yards of backing from my tested and trusted Islander reel . . .

I will be back—for more!

Barracuda—Marquesas—Florida

BARRAMUNDI— AUSTRALIA

Aussies just love to fish for barramundi—a close relative of the African Nile Perch. And for very good reasons. Barramundi are in many ways similar to American bass in that they are aggressive fish that strike hard and love to gobble surface flies and lures with their large underslung mouths. So, to an Aussie angler nothing quite compares to barra fishing!

Add to this that some of the world's best barramundi fishing is found near Darwin in the Northern Territory of Australia—"Top End of Down Under" as they jokingly say.

Here you will probably fish in the company of giant and dangerous man-eating saltwater crocodiles—Crocodile Dundee style. Always watch your back when you are on dry land—and always fish out of aluminum boats too large for a croc to attack them—meaning longer than 5 metres, longer than the crocs themselves. Only then are you safe. If only somewhat . . .

This particular barra was one out of a magnificent brace caught on fly and weighing close to 20 pounds each! They were the result of two intense days spent looking for the real trophies—neglecting all smaller fish that presented themselves.

BIG is beautiful—be it boats or barras!

Barramundi—Northern Territory—Australia

BLACKFIN TUNA—
FLORIDA

We all have our "fifteen minutes of fame"—at least according to avantgarde artist Andy Warhol. I think that I might have had my fifteen minutes of international fame one day while fishing the Gulf Stream out of Port Canaveral, Florida:

We were fishing with Capt. Mike who is a former demolition man and sargeant with the US Marines. He's got lower arms like Popeye and quite a temper . . .

With two 225HP Evinrudes on the transom and the 28 foot boat loaded with fuel like the nearby space shuttle—"90% fuel, 10% cargo"—we head out for the open ocean and the blue Gulf Stream running out here. We are looking for a shrimp boat that Mike has on the radar. A boat that has been fishing all night and now has sorted its catch and thrown out the excess.

Mike knows that boats like this one act like magnets on fish out here. They congregate behind and below the boats to feed on thrown out leftovers—and on smaller baitfish doing the same!

Capt. Mike is right. Immediately we hook into 3-5 kg bonitos that slam our dead drifted herrings. Soon after Mike also spots something bigger feeding deeper than the bonitos. He rigs another baitfish and lets it sink below the bonitos. Soon after he is rewarded with a heavy strike and a fight way harder than what the bonitos put up.

Up comes a mighty blackfin tuna of some 15 kg. An impressive adversary on light tackle. Then the rest of us also start hooking up and during the next two or three hours we do nothing but battle blackfins in the 10-15 kg range. What an afternoon!

We are tired, dried up and longing for a shower and a steak when we finish fishing and head back for Port Canaveral.

Then the phone rings. In the middle of the Gulf Stream! With land nowhere to be seen!

It's Capt. Mike who has been on the satellite phone back to Florida, telling a journalist from USA Today about this Danish group having a ball with blackfins.

Now the journalist wants to have *my* version of the story while we race back through the waves at 30 knots—55 kmph! Thus I get my fifteen minutes of fame, clinging to the boat with one hand while holding on to the sat phone with the other . . .

Next day, well rested from a good nights sleep, I go down to the newsstand to buy a copy. And there it is—our tuna trip making the front page of the local Florida section.

So I may never make it to the cover of the Rolling Stone. But I certainly made it to a section of USA Today!

Blackfin tuna—Port Canaveral—Florida

BLUEFISH—
NEW HAMPSHIRE

Bluefish—a favourite of former US presidents Bush, Senior as well as Junior—is a schooling fish that moves up and down the US eastcoast. Every spring it moves north and arrives at Martha's Vineyard in May where it will provide spectacular fishing on the open ocean.

Schools will usually consist of fish the same size and age but they will all be voracious feeders. Their razor sharp teeth will literally cut baitfish in two—leaving a very characteristic oil slick on the water. Hard to believe if you haven't seen it yourself.

This particular specimen was caught on my 40th birthday—in the middle of the Gulf Stream. I was visiting beautiful Martha's Vineyard where famous people (!) like to spend their spare time. Where notabilities can be seen walking the streets, safe from journalists and paparazzis.

I did too! Nobody noticed me. I had booked a couple of days of striped bass fishing but the fish had not arrived yet. We cast our flies over many good spots on the first day but didn't see a fish. On Day Two my guide suggested we go further out where the Gulf Stream picks up.

I couldn't believe my luck when we spotted sea gulls diving into the feeding frenzy caused by—the very first bluefish of the season! The first blues spotted that year off Martha's Vineyard. On my 40th birthday!

We hooked into several bluefish from several different schools before it was all over. The only signs of what had just happened?

Oil slicks covering the now smooth surface of the Gulf Stream . . .

Bluefish—Martha's Vineyard—Massachusetts

BLUE MARLIN—
CUBA

Battling a giant marlin has probably crossed the minds of most fishermen. But actually sitting there, attached to the colossal powers of a black, blue or striped marlin, is something out of this world. You seriously start to wonder who is battling who, and the outcome is never certain. You might be forced to give up . . .

I have been there only once, and the fish wasn't even a giant. It was a modest blue marlin of only 120 kg—some 264 lbs. But still the experience was overwhelming. Plus the fact that everything was just so visual.

After trolling for hours without seeing a fish, the Havanna skyline in the horizon being the only sign of life, a big brown shadow suddenly appeared behind the bait, a hand rigged squid. A few tense minutes followed while the long shape was inspecting our offer.

Everybody on board—captain, crew and fishermen—watched in awe as the fish finally made up its mind and whipped the squid out of the water with a fling of its long beak.

Immediately the captain stopped the boat, leaving the squid out there for the marlin to pick up. It seemed like forever before the fish returned. Its long beak completely out of the water it slowly rolled on the squid, dived and took off, the giant reel clicking loudly on a free spool.

—*Now!* called the captain.—*Strike!*

The brake was engaged and loose line reeled in. All of a sudden the weight of the giant fish became very real. Line raced off the reel as the fish lept and ran for life and for Florida.

I don't remember any real details from the fight, only that my arms were very sore the day after. After half an hour that seemed like forever, the blue marlin was ready to land. The shipmate grabbed the doubled leader and gaffed the tired fish. Then a lasso was put over its tail and the fish hauled on board.

Later, back at Hemingway Marina, our captain filleted a small white marlin that we also caught. We grilled some of it at a local restaurant, and it was great. Quite similar to veal steak. But most impressive was the full bottle of Cuban rum that he consumed while filleting the marlin . . .

BLUESTRIPE—
CUBA

The bony fishes comprise more than 30.000 species.

This means at least two things: That you will never catch them all. And that you will regularly catch some that you have never seen before—even if you are a fisheries biologist as I am!

A good friend and colleague of mine is a botanist and therefore very much into flowers. She tells me that when she was younger, she just had to determine the species of all the plants and flowers that she encountered. Quite tiring—even for a dedicated botanist . . .

Nowadays, she says that she is happy just looking at them, knowing full well that there will always be species she's never seen before and never will know about. In fact that has become an added attraction in itself—realizing that you don't know everything and don't have to!

I feel the same way about fish. These days I am happy to catch and admire a beautiful new fish species. I don't have to know it by its Latin name, realizing that it is but one of the 30.000 plus species found. I just relax and enjoy the colours.

You should too. This particular "bluestripe" was caught in the Jardines de la Reina National Park in southwestern Cuba. Old Fidel has assured that things here will remain the same for many years to come.

More power to him!

Bluestripe—Jardines de la Reina—Cuba

BONEFISH—
BRITISH VIRGIN ISLANDS

A lot of flyfishermen go through their lives without ever seeing their backing—except of course for the time when they actually loaded it on their reels . . .

Well, if that is the case with you, consider trying your luck at bonefishing. Bonefish are some of the strongest and certainly longest running fish that will ever grab your fly. Even a small 2 pounder is certain to go into your backing on its first run—not to mention what a large bonefish can do . . .

Add to this the fact that you will be fishing in beautiful tropical or subtropical surroundings—with coconut palms swaying in the wind on white and sandy coral beaches. The water is crystal clear and you will spot almost of all the fish you cast to. Visual fishing at is very best. And nothing prevents you from enjoying a Pinacolada or two when the day is done!

We spent two weeks walking down the Telegraph Road and wading up the Telegraph Beach in search of beautiful bonefish that averaged four pounds. Weather was not cooperative at all, big clouds hanging low and limiting our visibility.

Still we spotted, hooked and landed fish. But it turned out to be very much of a short range affair. Most fish were spotted so close in and so late that all it took was a short flip of the rod to bring your fly, leader and maybe a few yards of line into action. Takes were visible and action instant.

I managed to loose a large bone when my fly line got caught behind the reel seat. In a split second my leader snapped and the fish was gone . . .

That too is part of bonefishing!

Bonefish—Anegada—British Virgin Islands

BROOK TROUT— LABRADOR

Rarely do you catch big fish only when you fish dry flies only. But there are exceptions as I experienced myself one sunny day on Labrador's mighty Minipi Lake. I was guest at the Cooper's great Minipi Lodge here.

Weather had been horrible for weeks when all of a sudden the sky cleared and the wind came down. It didn't take long for the mayflies to realise that it was now or never this season. These giant mayflies should have hatched a full month ago but weather had been so miserable that they didn't.

Within an hour or so the mirror calm surface of the lake was covered with freshly hatched giant mayflies. In turn they were quickly detected by the giant brook trout living here. They had probably been waiting for them for as long as we flyfishermen had!

To make a long story short, I enjoyed a couple of hours of simply incredible dry fly fishing. It was out of this world. The smallest brook trout went 3 pounds—the largest 6. All on dry flies!

A strange thing happened though. My fishing partner Dave had his box full of giant #4 imitations so he was in for some serious action. At least we thought so. Fact was that he didn't catch a single fish. Fact also was that I hooked and landed one big brook trout after the other on a small #10 Adams Irresistable—fishing out of the same boat as Dave did with his seemingly perfect imitations.

Afterwards we came to the conclusion that it was the leader which made the difference. Not the fly. Dave had to use a very heavy tippet to effectively cast his large and bushy dry flies. Leaders that looked like pieces of rope on the mirror calm surface.

Whereas I could get by with a 4X tippet that didn't spook the hungry but still wary Minipi brook trout. A plausible explanation, I think.

After a few hours of hectic activity the sun disappeared behind thick clouds and the wind picked up again. The day ended with whitecapped waves rolling along the lake.

That day proved to be the only summer in Labrador that year . . .

Brook trout—Minipi Lake—Labrador

BROWN TROUT—
ARGENTINA

Sometimes you are just plain lucky to be in the right place at the right time—despite prevailing conditions.

This is exactly what happened to me one hot sommer day in the beautiful Los Alerces national park in Argentina. Here you can see the largest and oldest trees in the world, some having been here for 2.000 years!

We were sweating in the sun and just waiting for it to disappear behind the mountains—for the coolness of evening to replace it. Buses of school kids made good use of the warm weather though, basking in the sun and swimming in the river.

Drifting down a short stretch of running water connecting two lakes, I was casting a bushy dry fly towards a steep cliff dropping straight into the river—seemingly producing a bottomless hole—when a tiny shadow appeared from the bottom in the gin clear water. It grew bigger all the time, quite obviously targeting my fly.

It was engulfed in absolute slow motion and my strike was slow too. In fact so slow that my guide thought I hadn't seen the fish at all!

After feeling the hook the fish dove towards the bottom taking all of my flyline plus several yards of backing. First time ever that this has happened to me while dry fly fishing! And with the river bottom full of sunken logs, I figured that my chances of getting this fish to the boat were slim indeed.

Despite the tremendous pressure my 5X tippet held up, and after some serious pulling this beautiful 6 pound brown trout gave up and surfaced!

It was of course released back into its deep pool again. Afterwards we celebrated our good luck with a glass of chilled Chilean white wine—despite being in Argentina!

Some guys have all the luck . . .

Brown trout—Los Alerces—Argentina

BROWN TROUT—
CHILE

Chile is a long and narrow and fascinating country with loads of unspoilt nature, friendly people, great folklore and magnificent wine.

As for its geography, it bears great resemblance to Norway in Scandinavia, being long and narrow, north-south oriented with long fiords indenting the rocky coastline. It also offers a tremendous amount of good fishing opportunities—some of them yet to be explored.

This nice brown trout was taken in a Chilean mountain lake on a damselfly pattern. Evening fishing for large trout cruising around and chasing migrating damselflies was fantastic! No fish went smaller than 2 pounds and the largest going a full 6 pounds. Even this heavy-belllied, the browns were able to lift themselves completely out of the water during the fight!

Daytime was spent casting big bushy hoppers to openings in a small weed choked stream. None of the fish here were large—average being 35 cm—but fighting them in a stream with more weed than water presented problems that could only be solved by using heavy tippets and brute force.

Immediately upon setting the hook you had to pull them out of their holes and actually make them plane over the weed. Not very pretty to look at but quite exciting to experience!

Chile still offers the unspoilt trout fishing we all long for. The very same fishing that Argentina once did offer but no longer does.

Even a huge country like Argentina can get crowded and overfished in places. It might eventually happen to Chile too . . .

Brown trout—Balmaceda—Chile

BROWN TROUT II—
CHILE

Normally, you associate big fish with big water. But this isn't always so. Take for instance this brown trout which was caught in a brook that in places was no wider than my fly rod. Catching the amazingly large browns that live here requires no fancy casting. Casting simply isn't possible under such cramped conditions.

Instead you spot your fish and then you stalk them. When within fishing distance you either lob your weighted nymph in front of them or you lower your dry fly down on the water from a high vantage point. Then you watch the action!

Fighting big trout in a narrow and shallow burn is a mess. When hooked these fish will be thrashing wildly around, not knowing where to run or hide. Luckily—for them that is—there is always that submerged log or sunken tree to run for. And they do . . .

This particular brown trout was spotted and stalked from above. Then a big and bushy Stimulator dry fly was carefully lowered down into the mini canyon where the fish lurked. Watching it rise to the fly from above demanded the utmost in patience and restraint. Not until the fish had slowly gone down again, fly in its mouth, was it time to lift the rod and set the hook!

The fight that followed was crazy. Just getting down from the high cliff was enough to bring your adrenalin level to new heights! And then the big fish managed to wrap line and leader around a submerged log, seemingly lost for good.

Luckily, a diligent approach managed to free the leader and land the fish in the beginning dark. A few photos later the fish was allowed to slide back into its dark and mysterious pool. Probably very confused as to what had just happened. I was too.

And by the way: Getting up and out of the slippery canyon after the fight proved to be the biggest challenge of the day . . .

Brown trout—Coihaique—Chile

BROWN TROUT—
ICELAND

Iceland is a cold and barren country sometimes resembling the Moon. In fact, US astronauts have been trained here for that very reason!

But Iceland is made up of lava gulped out of the ocean bottom. This means that Icelandic rivers and lakes are very fertile—rich in nutrients and food. Combine this with the fact that water temperatures can be surprisingly high—due to geothermal activity—and you have the reason for the many healthy trout and salmon populations that Iceland is known for worldwide.

Salmon fishing in Iceland is expensive—bordering on the ridiculous. It has become the preferred passtime for the rich people of this world and accordingly the prices have sky rocketed. Today, peak season salmon fishing in a first class Icelandic river will cost you several thousand dollars . . .

But trout fishing is available to more people on a less expensive basis. And if you are willing to look around and travel long distances offroad, you may be rewarded with magnificent brown trout like this 9 pounder caught on fly in a remote mountain lake.

I was wading a shallow sand bank that led several hundred metres out into the lake, when I heard a big trout rolling on the surface—alas in the opposite end of the lake. But I was fortunate—or maybe it was another fish. Anyway, I had just put out a long line when suddenly, out of nowhere, a big swirl only few metres from my rod tip indicated that I was in the wrong direction.

Probably at the speed of sound, I managed to strip in my line and put my small Xmas Tree fly out where the fish had showed. My third pull resulted in a heavy strike and a big fish heading for the deep middle of the lake. Backing disappearing from my reel at an alarming rate, I tried to follow the fish but ended up in the middle of the lake where water got too deep.

Out here I had to fight the fish, and out here I had to land it. No net at hand and nowhere to beach the fish, I had to grab it over the neck and carry it ashore. I was in a killing mood so dispatched the fish when I reached shore. It provided great Xmas eating when it was later smoked!

Brown trout—Veidivötn—Iceland

COBIA—
FLORIDA

On a cold winter's day I decided to migrate southwest to Key West, Florida which is an amazing place to be.

I was going fishing for barracuda and I was also exploring the previous fishing waters of famous writer Ernest Hemingway, casting big poppers to sunken logs visible on the bottom of the clear water. Every now and then a log moved around and turned into a 10-20 pound barracuda—fast as lightning!

In the afternoon the weather grew worse and we decided to head back in. When all of a sudden a school of large dark fish appeared. They looked like shark to me but my guide immediately identified them as cobia. They were spooky, milling around and difficult to reach in the wind that was picking up. Whenever we closed in on them, they moved away just a bit further.

But finally I managed my best cast ever and landed the big Cockroach fly just on the edge of the school. The very limit of my casting skills. The fly was taken immediately and a long and hard fight followed. The fish was a cobia of some 22 pounds and it was realeased to join its school again.

—*It was a keeper*, my guide said.—*The size limit here is 30 inches and it was well above that . . .*

A well chosen and rather grown up size limit, I must say!

Cobia—Key West—Florida

COMMON CARP— DENMARK

Carp are many things and carp are viewed in many different ways, depending on where you are and what you want from them.

In China they farm them on the rice fields and eat them with great appetite. In southern Europe they raise them in ponds and eat them for Christmas—made "blue" by pouring boiling vinegar over them before serving. And in the US of A they curse them—especially the silver carp—for infesting the waters around the Great Lakes to such an extent that you can be hit by a frightened flying carp when you go by one in a boat . . .

On the opposite, in England common carp are held in high esteem by dedicated carp fishermen who go to great length to catch one. Killing one and eating it just isn't done. You will get into serious trouble if you do so in the UK. Here they are all released to fight again. Here carp fishermen sleep out in bivvy sacks and mix their own "boilies" from very, very secret ingredients. Some even say that the best boilies are cooked around midnight on a full moon . . .

Well, to each his own, and carp are often looked down upon by flyfishermen in pursuit of trout and salmon. But for no good reasons. In fact carp are very challenging opponents on a fly rod, and once fooled into hitting your fly, common carp are very strong fish to battle and land. Quite often you will experience runs longer than the ones you get from trout and salmon!

This particular carp was spotted vacuum cleaning the muddy bottom in very shallow water. It took a small #8 fly dressed heavily so that it wouldn't sink into the mud. To help avoid that it was also suspended below a small foam strike indicator.

This fish proved beyond any doubt that handling a heavy carp in a small canoe is no mean task. Especially when you have to turn around to smile to the photographer . . .

Common carp—Bay of Mariager—Denmark

DORADO—
ARGENTINA

"Dorado" means "gold" in Spanish and the South American fish bearing the same name certainly lives up to that. It is probably the most sought after game fish in all of South America, living in the fast flowing rivers of Argentina and neighbouring countries.

Dorado are broadbacked, strong and aggressive fish with an adipose fin—despite the fact that they are in no way related to trout and salmon of the Northern hemisphere. They behave like a mixture of bass and trout in that they hold in the same places as do trout—and strike with the same ferocity as do bass!

Thus they are great game fish that strike hard and put up a good fight with the occasional leap thrown in. Most large specimens will show signs of fin clipping—performed by specialized piranhas too small to eat the fish itself but large enough to sneak up on a dorado and take a bite of its tail!

So, when fighting a big dorado, you will often notice the smaller piranhas chasing its tail and trying to bite pieces out of it. Imagine being the mighty dorado who normally rules the river. And who all of a sudden has to fight the fisherman and fight off the piranhas—at the same time . . .

This particular dorado was caught on a large black Muddler thrown into a back eddy of a beautiful and meandering river in northern Argentina. It weighed well over 10 pounds and was released to fight again.

So, if you are a gold digger, this part of the world is a must. Here the gold has fins and swims!

Dorado—Parana River—Argentina

DORADO—
MEXICO

The Sea of Cortez between the Baja peninsula and mainland North America was named after the Spanish conquerer bearing the same name. It is a very deep ocean that offers beautiful fishing in its clear and cobolblue waters.

If you are surface oriented and a flyfisherman, casting floating poppers on a floating line over very, very deep water may be just the right thing for you. You will be targeting dorado—also known as dolphin though no whale relation—that swim around in schools looking for anything that floats in the ocean.

Weed, timber or plastic boxes—anything afloat will attract baitfish looking for shade and shelter in the blistering sun. There is nothing else out here so any kind of shelter will do—artificial or not. The baitfish in turn will attract the dorados that you are looking for.

If fish are present, fishing is easy. Often the eager dorados will fight each other to get the fly, and it is not uncommon for one dorado to grab the fly that another dorado just threw in a summersaulting leap. Or to grab it out of the mouth of one already hooked! These fish love to fly, and they jump like butterflies, flapping around in midair!

This particular dorado took a popper, flapped around in midair a few times before it dove for the depths, leaving the fisherman with all of his flyline and one hundred yards of backing pointing straight towards the bottom. It took an additional ten minutes to bring the fish back up . . .

Filleted, dorados make very good eating and so did this one. It was barbecued and eaten back at the hotel in the evening, a

Mexican brass band playing the same four tunes over and over again . . .

Luckily, a good supply of tasty Mexican "XX" beer kept us in good spirit—and from stopping them!

Dorado—Cabo San Lucas—Mexico

EUROPEAN GRAYLING— DENMARK

Grayling are members of the salmon family but they look very different from the better known trout and salmon. In fact they look a lot more like their close cousins, the whitefish. Both have the small adipose fin characteristic of all true salmonoid fishes.

There are but two species of grayling—the Arctic and the European grayling. European grayling typically inhabit the lower and slower stretches of running water where they often outcompete trout.

For that reason they are often looked upon as thrash fish that should be removed from popular trout streams. In many English chalk streams that is the case. Here grayling are sometimes even netted to keep the population down and reduce competition with brown trout stocks.

Trout on the other hand are the king of fast flowing rivers further up in the mountains. Here the weaker grayling cannot compete or handle the swift currents that would quickly wash them away. Trout are much stronger.

Grayling are appropriately called "the queen of the river" as they are very feminine in both appearance and behaviour. In the German Rhine area the saying goes that *"Asch ist der Rhein Graf, Salm nur ein Herr"*. Which is German for *"grayling being the Count of the river whereas salmon are but the peasants"* . . .

No matter how you look upon grayling, they are THE perfect fish for flyfishermen preferring dry flies. No matter how the conditions, well almost, grayling can be enticed to rise to the surface to suck down a floating fly.

Grayling just love to rise to the surface to engulf floating insects—and artificial flies. So we let them!

European grayling—River Guden—Denmark

HALIBUT—
GREENLAND

Halibut are huge, magnificent and mysterious fishes—the stuff legends are made of!

Halibut live in the depths of the oceans—often down to 300 metres. But occasionally, during the short Arctic summer, they will seek refuge in shallow water. Here they will look for locations where the bottom is made up of shingle, gravel or clay—typically places with some current passing over them.

This is when and where they will become accessible to anglers seeking the thrill of hooking up with the biggest of all flounders. Here they can be caught on light tackle in water often shallower than 10 metres.

When you hook them this shallow, they will put up a tremendous fight making long runs, surfacing and diving again. They have no swim bladder and thus can move up and down in the water column as they like. When you hook them in deeper water, they are immediately given away by their characteristic undulating body movements. You always know when you hook one!

The Greenland halibut pictured here weighed in at 21 kg's and was caught on a shallow clay bank in the Godthaab Fiord. It was clearly visible from the boat in no more than 8 metres of water and made several passes at the lure before it finally attacked to kill. What a thrill!

Unfortunately for it, halibut have white meat and are great to eat. So it was the halibut itself that got killed. Shot with a .22 rifle to calm it down before landing . . .

Halibut—Nuuk—Greenland

HUMPBACK SALMON—
ALASKA

Atlantic salmon are magnificent creatures that demand the greatest respect and admiration. Salmo the Leaper has caught the attention of human kind since the Romans first saw it and named it on the Rhine, some 2.000 years ago. Salmo Salar—Salmo the Leaper.

Pacific salmon are even more fascinating in that they show tremendous difference between the species and undergo amazing changes in appearance once they leave the ocean and head for the spawning grounds. They undergo a kind of metamorphosis, changing them from one specialised fish into another equally specialized.

Out in the ocean all five species look somewhat similar with their torpedo shaped silvery bodies. But once they mature and migrate back to their river of birth—something they accomplish with amazing precision—the silvery Pacific salmon undergo a complete metamorphosis. Their loose silvery scales give way to a thickened slimy skin that turns into darker colors, specific to each species.

The fish pictured here is a male humpback salmon that has been in the river for a while but is not yet on the spawning grounds. It has changed from a silvery torpedo into a grotesque humpback creature with huge jaws, protruding teeth and an aggressive behaviour.

The females undergo a similar color change but stay within the slim torpedo body. Obviously they know better than the males how to keep their good looks!

Humpback salmon—Iliamna Lake—Alaska

JACK CREVALLE—
COSTA RICA

Jack Crevalle are some of the strongest fish that swim. Anyone who has actually played one will testify to that.

But anyone who claims to have played a Jack Crevalle to exhaustion—is a bloody liar! These fish just never give up. In this respect they are similar to arctic char—albeit much faster and way stronger. Many tropical fish have powers out of this world—a fact closely related to the significantly higher metabolism of tropical fish compared to fish in colder climates.

This gives them the power to just run and run and run. And this is where you badly need that reel which can "stop a train"—as 3M once advertised their new System Two reels as being capable of!

This particular Jack took my big white Whistler fly while I was casting to rolling tarpon off the mouth of Rio Colorado i Costa Rica. It caught me off guard as I had momentarily released the brake pressure set by my guide for tarpon—simply to be able to strip line off the reel at all for casting. I had just lowered my rod after delivering and was about to tighten the drag again when a fish hit.

The Jack struck megahard and ran off leaving me with a wildly spinning spool and the handle hitting my knuckles several times in the process. To make things even worse, when I was about to boat it, my beefy class 12 broke with a mighty bang . . .

Thus I have the greatest respect for Jacks of any kind—especially the mighty Crevalle!

Jack Crevalle—Colorado River—Costa Rica

JACK CREVALLE—
CUBA

I had caught Jack Crevalle before—even large specimens—but never on poppers. When fishing Jardines de la Reina in Cuba in 2009, we experienced a spell of bad weather coming in from the north.—*Those gringos never bring any good*, my guide grumbled, as both tarpon and bonefish had left the shallow flats in search of deeper and warmer waters.

Luckily, my guide knew what to put instead. In howling winds we were prowling the leeside of bays looking for sardines stacked up there. They were given away by the pelicans diving into the schools and filling their big beaks. Once located the sardines would hold the key to where the big barracudas and the odd Jack Crevalle would be lurking.

And once spotted, it was a matter of quick fire casting to dark shadows appearing over the light sandy bottom. If your popper landed too close, even the biggest barracuda would spook and run for cover. But presented correctly, a few metres in front of the fish, your popper would trigger a lightning fast strike that would litterally yank the rod out of your hand if you didn't hold on to it for life!

Occasionally a small group of speedy Jack Crevalles would swim by, offering you a very short window of opportunity to get their attention. Takes were almost faster than the ones of barracuda and the following fight longer than anything I had ever experienced with fish this size.

Jack Crevalle just don't give in. You have to force them in. Landing the specimen pictured here—on heavy 12 weight tackle—required almost half an hour of intensive battle . . .

It was killed and brought back to our hotel boat where it provided food for the entire crew. It definitely died for a reason!

Jack Crevalle—Jardines de la Reina—Cuba

KING SALMON—
ALASKA

The king salmon truly lives up to his name. He IS the king of all salmon! Simply being the biggest of all the 5 (6 in Asia) Pacific salmon species earns him the title.

Giants in the 40 kg class are known but today 30 kg is a more likely upper limit. 20 kg specimens are caught on a regular basis and in many places the average weight is around 25 pounds, smaller kings locally being called "jack salmon" instead of kings.

This is an important attraction to fishermen who travel to Alaska from all over the world. In Alaska you will almost certainly catch salmon. And if you fish for king salmon at the right time in the right place, you will almost certainly catch fish—and BIG fish only!

If you want to catch the biggest king salmon fresh and silvery from the ocean, you have to concentrate on the lower reaches of the bigger rivers. This calls for heavy tackle. On the other hand, if you have always wanted to do battle with a 40 or 50 pounder on your single handed fly rod, opt for the smaller rivers and tributaries further upstream. Here it is often visual fishing where you stalk single fish and cast to them specifically.

This particular 40 pound king salmon was caught on fly—single handed—in the Susitna River near Iliamna, Alaska. It was holding besides a sunken log and was clearly visible in the water.

The fight was mean and dirty—as the fish itself . . .

King salmon—Susitna River—Alaska

LARGEMOUTH BASS— CUBA

Cuba means Fidel Castro, Ernest Hemingway, pretty women, strong rum, big cigars and Big Game. Loads of marlin are caught each year in the "Blue River" off Cuba—in the Gulf Stream at depths of more than 2.000 metres. Fishing is done with the few skyscrapers of downtown Havana as a natural backdrop.

But originally, Cuba also held healthy populations of largemouth bass that could be a real challenge when you have to pull them out of the brackish mangroves! Obviously these areas provide plenty of food making for fast growth of the largemouth bass that often grew into double-digit weights.

For some years now American citizens have not been allowed to visit Cuba—for political reasons. But quite a few hardy US fishermen have overcome this obstacle by travelling to Cuba from neighbouring Canada or Mexico. Stories of huge largemouth Cuban bass have been just too tempting for these gentlemen . . .

Unfortunately and of lately, the Cuban bass populations have suffered from the invasion of other species—to the extent that Cuban bass fishing is not at all what it used to be. The 6 pound largemouth pictured here is thus becoming a thing of the past.

Maybe unfortunately too, Americans have now been allowed to travel to Cuba as they like. Courtesy of the Obama administration. This will certainly put a lot of strain on the local economy—and on the Cuban way of communism too.

I wonder how old Fidel and his younger brother Raoul will handle that . . .

Largemouth bass—Laguna de la Leche—Cuba

LENOK—
SIBIRIA

When fishing in Sibiria you will almost certainly come across the lenok—the most abundant salmonoid in this part of the world. You will quickly learn to appreciate it as it will make up a substantial part of your diet—especially if you are on a float trip where you cannot bring a lot of food.

If you are a fisheries biologist as I am, the lenok has an added attraction: It is a strange fish bearing resemblance to almost all other trout and salmon of this world. It has the soft head and mouth of a grayling. It has the tiny scales and white fin trims of a char. And it has the dark spots of the trout and salmon. This has given rise to speculations that lenok might indeed be the true forefathers of all trout and salmon.

Whether this is true or not has yet to be determined. In the meantime you might want to watch this gentle and softmouthed fish feed in the shallows. Like its big brother, the mighty taimen, lenok also love tasty rodents. But unlike the taimen who is able to drown even the biggest rodent with a slab of its giant tail, the smaller lenok have to resort to other and more subtle tactics:

When they spot a swimming mouse, they gently approach it and start pulling its legs to drown it. They will continue doing this for quite some time, if need be. Imagine being the mouse in that situation . . .

And whereas the lenok is certainly pulling the legs of swimming mice, I am definitely not pulling yours!

—Drama at its best!

Lenok—Lena River—Sibiria

MACHAKA—
COSTA RICA

When you have just emptied your wallet to go tarpon fishing in Costa Rica, you might want to concentrate on just that: Tarpon.

But you should have an open mind and not let your guide down the day he suggests that instead you go upriver and cast poppers for something called "machaka". You will be in for a lot of fun if you follow his suggestion and leave the tarpon for a while. Hopefully you have already landed a few silvery giants which will make you more relaxed!

Machaka are distantly related to piranhas but feed primarily on fruits and prey that drop down on the water from surrounding trees. Good spots accordingly have deep holding water, steep banks and overhanging branches. Drop that fly in between the branches and if machaka are present, strikes will be immediate.

Don't leave your fly floating for more than a few seconds—it is the "plop on the drop" that triggers the strike. Not the float iself as is normally the case with regular dry flies. You are just wasting prescious fishing time floating that fly! Instead: Cast, cast, cast . . .

This particular machaka was caught in the upper Rio Colorado after a long day's fishing and litterally thousands of casts.

Boy, that wrist was sore . . .

Machaka—Rio Colorado—Costa Rica

MANGROVE JACK—
AUSTRALIA

If you are poling the shallow mangroves of northern Australia, chances are that you will come across a mangrove jack eagerly ambushing your fly or lure—in the process doing serious damage to it with its sharp teeth.

I always associate mangrove jacks with mud crabs—and the sound of them. Explanation: When I first visited the "Top End of Down Under", I was just so jetlagged. When I arrived at the camp—after more then 24 hours of continuous travel—I fell asleep immediately. When I woke up again, the first I heard was the continuous heavy pounding on something hard that cracked.

It took me almost an hour to wake up sufficiently, get up and get dressed. When I made it to the kitchen, I got the explanation. There—benched around a big table—sat three stocky Aussies, each with a heavy metal stick in his hands. On the table lay the freshly crushed shells of more mud crabs than I could count. They all looked happy—the Aussies that is—and they all raised their beer to greet me.

—*Would you like some mud crab for breakfast?*

No thank you. I am not really into crabs and shellfish—especially not for breakfast. So I got a freshly fried mangrove jack instead—served with a cool beer, of course. I still wonder if that is what Aussies always have for breakfast:—Mud crab and beer?

Anyway, the mangrove jack proved to be great eating, and before I left I had eaten quite a few of them. It looks frightening with its sharp dog-like teeth but the meat is just so tasty. Not at all like mud crab. So when inspecting the crab traps on our way home in the evening, we always put in a little popper fishing for mangrove jacks.

Tasty and entertaining at the same time!

Mangrove Jack—Northern Territory—Australia

MULLET—
DENMARK

Mullet are strange game fish in the sense that they are strictly vegetarians. They feed almost exclusively on floating or attached algae making them very difficult to catch on conventional tackle. It is just so hard trying to imitate microscopic algae . . .

Luckily, every now and then mullet loose their mind and start chasing bigger prey. As any normal predatory fish would. When this happens you may be lucky enough to hook and land one of these impressive fighters. You certainly don't have to be a meat eater to be a strong fighter!

Mullet are newcomers to Scandinavia where I caught this one. They have arrived with the global warming of the oceans, in a few years establishing strong native stocks up here. On a peculiar note, I once managed to hook and land a small yellowspotted mullet when fishing for sea bass off the coast of Jersey in the British Channel.

Catching it was pure luck—I readily admit that—but I was even luckier than that: This particular fish put me on the front page of the angling news in the local newspaper!

Obviously it was quite a rare catch. And I just thought that it was cute . . .

Mullet—Bay of Randers—Denmark

MUTTON SNAPPER—
BELIZE

My alltime fishing idol, Lefty Kreh, once wrote that mutton snappers are some of the hardest fish to catch on the flats and on flies.

Well, I am not one to question Lefty's statements and luckily, there are always exceptions to the rule. Even to what Lefty says.

Years ago, I was touring Central America with a girlfriend and finally, we ended up in beautiful Ambergris Caye in Belize. Stepping out of the banana boat which took us there, we were greeted by frigate birds diving for baitfish. A most promising welcome!

One sunny day we booked a young local guide who came highly recommended by some Americans we had met earlier on. He was certainly a good fishing guide but he wasn't very communicative. In fact he hardly spoke the whole day—except for the occasional *"Bonefish—12 o'clock—20 yards"* stuff that all fishermen like to hear.

After nailing a few bones on small Crazy Charlies we decided it was time for a lunch break—and a swim in the beautiful bluegreen channel between two small mangrove islands. The crystal clear water was just too tempting and the midday sun too hot.

Our guide didn't like that one bit. He thought we were on a fishing trip—not swimming and snorkeling. He was disappointed, to say the least. We had turned out to be just another pair of bloody tourists . . .

Anyway, we enjoyed our lunch and a great channel swim before crawling back on board and picking up the fly rod again. Then I spotted a fish moving along the banks of the channel, put a white Clouser out in front if it and immediately hooked it.

Well, you have probably guessed it by now: It turned out to be a fine mutton snapper which put up a nice fight before being landed, photographed and released back into the channel.

And the morale? There is always a lucky shot to even the most difficult of fish. I am sure Lefty agrees. I am also certain that he is not offended. 'Cause he knows better than most!

Mutton snapper—Ambergris Caye—Belize

PACIFIC SAILFISH—
PANAMA

Probably the biggest feat that I've ever accomplished—landing a fish longer than myself and my fly rod!

This particular fish was my first Pacific sailfish caught off the coast of Panama. It was one out of seven fish that I brought to the boat for tagging and release that week. All fish were 100 pound+ and around 10 feet long. Amazing.

First you tease these fish to the boat and then you throw a huge popper out in front of them. Then you strip the fly and wait for the sailfish to turn around and pounce upon the fly. The best part: You get to watch the giant fish—all lit up in purple colors from sheer excitement—come down on the fly, its long beak out of the water . . .

Finally, you have to wait for it to go down again before you hit it. Hard. Down and dirty. Several times. If he is not headed in the right direction, you simply cannot get a strong enough hook hold.

Then it is time to clear all the loose line that is lying on the deck. In a few seconds all line will be cleared by the fish in its first long run—if it doesn't get tangled up somewhere. Then even the strongest tippet will not be strong enough . . .

After the initial bewilderment from feeling the hook the sail just strips 200 or even 300 yards of line from your reel, leaving your body sweating and your heart pounding!

The worst part is reeling back hundreds of yards of backing—just to see it disappear again. And again.

Still—this kind of fishing is strangely addictive. Don't ask me why . . .

Pacific sailfish—Pinas Bay—Panama

PACU—
PERU

People tend to think of piranhas as aggressive, bloodthirsty beasts that will eat anything alive. And rightly so with smaller species like the redbellied piranha who—for that specific purpose—has razorsharp teeth. They can be as dangerous as you can imagine!

But few people know that even the much feared redbellied piranha is normally a very shy creature which spooks easily and does its best to get out of your way—when not in that feeding frenzy. Not until it has been turned on, is the redbellied piranha of any danger to its surroundings.

Even fewer people know that the much feared piranha has a close cousin which is a dedicated vegetarian! I am talking about the stocky pacu which grows to several kg's on a diet of mostly fruits crunched with its strong molar teeth. This diet produces some very tasty meat making the pacu a very popular fish with the local indians.

Luckily, the pacu doesn't mind a meaty snack from time to time. Thus, occasionally it will strike a lure in between all the vegetables—as did this particular 5 kg fish which didn't live to tell.

It provided ample food for all of us that evening!

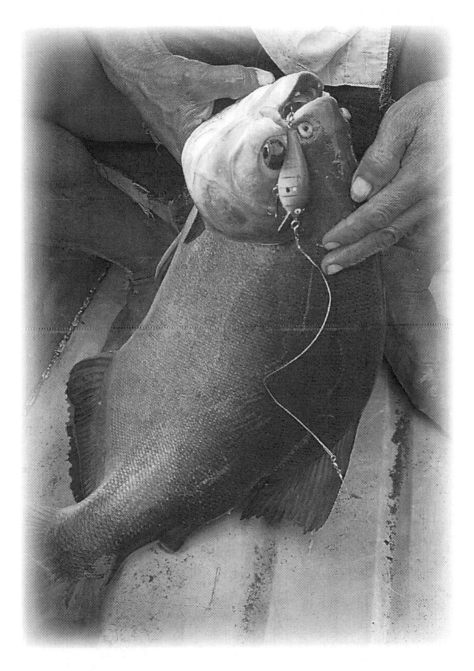

Pacu—Amazon River—Peru

PEACOCK BASS—
ECUADOR

All bass are magnificent game fish in their own right but the peacock bass of the Amazon River basin is definitely the gamest—by a very wide margin. It is extremely aggressive, highly territorial and a voracious feeder that will throw itself on anything that moves—if in the mood for that!

Add to this that peacock bass are just so beautiful with their bright red and orange colours contrasting their green and bronze bodies. Plus they are stronger than you can possibly imagine before hooking one!

I lost my first half a dozen peacocks before I realized that you have use way heavier tackle than you normally would for a fish this size. And a lot of brute force too. Otherwise you don't stand a chance of keeping hooked fish out of the branches where they lurk.

I vividly remember how my sweaty hands couldn't grip the flyline firmly enough. No matter how hard I squeezed the line, the peacocks managed to rip it out of my grip. So initially, they won all the battles. Bar none.

Later I learned to angle my hand in addition to gripping the line as firmly as I possibly could. You have to apply all the pressure you can upon hooking one. Otherwise you will just end up with your line completely tangled up in the jungle . . .

For these reasons the peacock bass of the Amazon is very high on my own Top Ten list of game fish species. Probably in the Top Three!

Peacock bass—Amazon River—Ecuador

PERCH—
DENMARK

Danish perch are great fish in all respects. They are beautiful fish with their orange fins, green backs and black stripes. In many ways they resemble the mighty peacock bass of the Amazon.

Perch can be finicky and tricky to catch, as their mood is very dependent upon barometric pressure. This is due to the simple fact that they have a closed swim bladder and therefore need time to adjust the internal pressure. If the barometer suddenly drops, perch will loose interest in feeding and consequently get difficult to catch.

But once caught, no other fish tastes as well. Being an old time fan of European perch, I thoroughly enjoyed one particular fishing trip with famous Danish TV personality Poul Thomsen on the Bay of Randers.

Poul is also very fond of catching perch and loves to eat them as well. We spent one glorious October day pursuing these striped critters and had great luck casting soft tail jigs to them.

We almost filled the boat with sizable perch culminating with this grand specimen weighing in at 1,55 kg and measuring 48 cm. My biggest perch so far though I have caught plenty of 1 kg+ fish.

Poul netted the fish for me and took the photo. Afterwards we had a great dinner of freshly caught, cleverly cut and delicately fried perch fillets at his house in Albæk overlooking the bay.

What a great day that was!

Perch—Bay of Randers—Denmark

PERCH II—
DENMARK

If you are a fly fisherman, the heat of summer usually means that you will spend your time on different pastimes. Trout and salmon fishing will be off in the heat and you might as well take up swimming or other water sports—while waiting for the water to cool down again.

Enter once again the magnificent European perch which just happens to love warm water. In fact it seems to get more active and surface-oriented the warmer the water gets. Combine this with the fact that perch love to gobble up anything that breathes and moves, and you have a winning combination.

Big bushy flies usually do the trick—small poppers too. So pick up your fly rod and go to a nearby lake to cast your flies in the heat of summer. You may want to leave your waders back home. Provided of course the sun is out and about. Otherwise you might have to put on some extra layers to stay warm. After all, it is Scandinavia . . .

No matter what you do, be sure to enjoy the summer and the perch fillets that you may bring home. Nothing is tastier than a freshly caught perch—be it fried, steamed or even smoked.

We once smoked a batch of freshly caught perch during a TV shoot. Both the head photographer and the sound engineer were delighted and put in some extra work that day!

As always: You have to feed them, fish as well as photographers, to keep them happy . . .

Perch—River Guden—Denmark

PIKE—
DENMARK

There is something deeply fascinating and at the same time very scary about pike—the only freshwater crocodile that we have here in Europe!

This impression is strengthened by the simple fact that all pike have some 8.000 sharp teeth in their mouths. If you don't believe me, do feel free to count yourself!

Its sneaky way of ambushing its prey is exhilarating and makes for some great visual flyfishing. There is nothing quite like seeing a monster pike attack your floating popper and watch it disappear in a mighty swirl! It looks as if someone just pulled the plug in the lake . . .

Add to this the fact that pike grow to large sizes rarely reached by other freshwater fish and you have the reason for its popularity with all kinds of fishermen. 10 kg pike are not uncommon and are caught on a regular basis. 15 kg seems to be a magical mark seldom reached—despite the fact that pike may grow bigger than 30 kg . . .

This particular 10 kg+ pike was caught on Opening Day, May 1st, in Danish Lake Fussing. It was a heavy female, its belly full of roe and ready to spawn. We saw it follow our flies several times before it finally decided to take.

It inhaled a monstrous Flash fly in very shallow water. When trying to net it, my friend broke his landing net by the handle . . .

Stories like that add to the pike's reputation as a cruel dude!

Pike—Lake Fussing—Denmark

PIKE II—
DENMARK

Back in 1974 I had hit upon a small pond near my parents' place that housed some amazingly large pike. I started out with a nice fish of some 6 kg and finished off with this beautiful specimen weighing exactly 11 kg, caught in the very same pond two years later.

I say exactly, as it was weighed on a certified scale at the nearby post office. This was important to me as in those days I was hunting for my first ever Gold Needle from Swedish tackle manufacturer ABU Garcia and thus needed the official documentation from a certified scale!

Pike are fascinating fish and catching a true monster like this in a pond that you can cover with a decent spinning cast—is even more fascinating. They look monstruous in that small a piece of water. Reaching such a size means that over the years, they have gobbled up just about everything that swims or flies in that particular pond—fish, frogs, ducks, mice etc.

This 11 kg pike swallowed an 18 gram ABU Reflex revolving spoon as its last meal. I have caught a lot of pike on that particular spinner which is still a firm favourite with me and many other fishermen here in Scandinavia. The 7 and 12 gram versions are great spinners for perch too.

I brought the big pike home across the handlebars of my green Puch Maxi moped, parading the neighborhood very slowly, making sure that everybody had seen my freshly caught trophy!

When I rang the door bell at my parents' house, my mother opened the door very slowly and looked out through a narrow gap.

—*Now what are you bringing home this time?* she whispered, having received a small shock the last time I brought home a monster pike . . .

Pike—Nordborg—Denmark

PIRANHA—
PERU

Very few people—be they fishermen or not, men, women or children—haven't heard of the bloodthirsty piranhas of the Amazon jungle.

Fish that will rip off all the flesh of an unfortunate cow or horse in mere minutes. Fish that enter a collective feeding frenzy once they smell the blood and face the competition from fellow piranhas.

But it is little known that the much feared redbellied piranha actually is a very shy fish that hides and flees instead of standing up and fighting. Mostly, piranhas will spook when disturbed—a behaviour far from their better known aggressive way of feeding.

Still, the stories about their razorsharp teeth are absolutely correct. When flyfishing for piranhas or other species, the piranhas will trim your Muddler flies with more proficiency than you could ever do yourself—even with the best pair of scissors!

Those triangular teeth cut through everything, leaving your fly box a mere shadow of its former self. When casting big flies for golden dorados, I have often witnessed how coloured feathers all of a sudden came drifting down with the current. Now where did they come from?

When I inspected my fly, its tail was gone. Completely. And I never felt a thing. Not even the slightest pull.

Those piranha teeth *are* razor sharp . . .

Piranha—Parana River—Argentina

PIRARA—
ECUADOR

The redtail catfish is one of the prettier species that you are likely to catch if you go fishing in the Amazon area of South America. The mighty Amazon houses a lot of different species of catfish—some small, some large and some even poisonous.

You are also likely to hear the redtail catfish before you actually see it. Often you will be able to determine what is on your hook when the fish is still deep down in the water: A pirara as the locals call it.

The explanation behind this unusual phenomenon is the fact that piraras use their highly developed swimbladder to make loud humming or drumming noises that are easily heard in the murky water—and above. Once hooked, they grunt loudly to tell you and the rest of the world that they are not at all happy with the situation!

But don't be afraid. Piraras are friendly fish that have no bad intentions whatsoever. They are not poisonous. They do not sting. And they don't look ugly. In fact they look pretty good . . .

Just enjoy their vivid coloration, pat them on the back or kiss them goodbye before you return them to their beloved Amazon River.

Then you've got a friend!

Pirara—Amazon River—Ecuador

POISONFISH—
MEXICO

In some areas top predators like barracuda and others are poisonous and will cause "ciguatera" in those who eat them. You will be very sick and you may get high fever. Eventually, you may die.

This poison is accumulated by coral algae and passed on through the food chain, finally ending up in the meat of the barracuda where it may reach dangerously high concentrations. Enough to kill as no effective antidote is known.

Other fish species are directly poisonous in that they produce the poison themselves and have spines to spread it. The deadliest one is that master of camouflage, the rockfish, which lives in shallow water where you might actually step on him.

If you do, you are not likely to forget the experience. In a worst case scenario you will die but if you don't, you will experience the worst kind of pain that can be inflicted upon a human being. That's what survivors of its sting tell. It is that bad.

Well, luckily it doesn't have to be deadly when you encounter a poisonous fish. This particular species has two sharp belly spines that will cause a lot of pain and keep you away from fishing for hours and even days, depending on your allergic reaction.

I was just about to grab it when my guide cried out a loud warning: *"No, no, senor—peligroso!"*—which means "dangerous" in Spanish.

So, if you don't recognize the fish species you just caught:
—Don't touch it!

Poisonfish—Sian Kaan—Mexico

POLLACK—
NORWAY

Pollack are great fish on a fly rod. They strike hard and they dive hard. Their initial run is close to unstoppable and great fun. Despite this, pollack are much overlooked by fly fishermen who spend most of their time looking and fishing for trout and salmon—often catching none . . .

When salmon fishing in Norway you will be presented with all sorts of excuses for the bad fishing you are experiencing. The water may be too high or too low, too warm or too cold, too clear or too murky. The previous winter may have been too dry, resulting in too little runoff at snow melt. Or the river may run too high due to excessive precipitation.

You never know the reason why you are not catching anything but it happens all the time. Never will they tell you that the real reason lies in the numerous illegal nets in the nearby fiord. Or local environmental issues like damming, digging, clear cutting etc. But always: You should have been here last year or last week . . .

Enter the mighty pollack. In most nearby fiords there will be plenty of mackerel and pollack to compensate even the most blasé and skunked fly fisherman. You throw out your fly and let it sink in eager anticipation of the strike to come. You smile when you hear your reel screaming during that first run, and you enjoy the tasty fillets in the evening.

Then you think of the price you have just paid for this action packed adventure: Nothing. Absolutely nothing. This fishing is free! Absolutely free! You might also happen to compare it to what you paid for your fishless week up in the river . . .

This particular pollack was caught on a skerry off the Norwegian island of Smøla. It took a bright white bucktail which was cast almost onto the skerry seen in the background and left to sink on a T-500 very fast sinking line before being retrieved back into deeper water.

The initial run was into the backing. Now, how many salmon could have done that?

Pollack—Smøla—Norway

QUEENFISH—
AUSTRALIA

Northern Australia's queenfish is a much overlooked game fish. In fact most people have never heard of them.

Queenfish provide spectacular action once you find them, stripping line from your reel at blistering speeds, jumping out of the water and flapping around in midair like a butterfly. Not unlike a summersaulting dorado.

Plus it has that pre-historic look to it that many Australian fish species have! A look that tells a long story about Australia having been isolated from the rest of the world for so long that many species have originated down here that do not exist anywhere else. Indigenous stuff like the Australian aboriginals themselves!

Only one bad thing comes to mind when speaking of northern Australia and that is the climate. Terrible. Very, very hot. But worst of all: An air humidity around 100%. All the time. Something which makes efficient sweating impossible. You sweat, yes. But sweat just sticks to you and you feel wet all the time—because you are!

Add to this the fact that you are fishing in Crocodile Dundee territory. You should always watch your back for big saltwater crocs sneaking up on you when you are occupied casting your flies to big barras, serious saratoga—or the queenfish in question . . .

Apart from that, fishing "down under" is simply amazing!

Queenfish—Northern Territory—Australia

RAINBOW TROUT—
ALASKA

Rainbow trout are some of the most sought after game fish in the world. For many good reasons: They are great fighters that love to jump out of the water while fighting for their lives.

Alaska is famous for its large rainbow trout which are in fact not trout but a close relative to the many Pacific salmon it lives among. Rainbow trout are related to Pacific salmon the same way as European brown trout are related to Atlantic salmon. So—if you think that the rainbow is a trout, you are terribly mistaken! But it certainly looks like a trout . . .

The really big rainbow trout of Alaska are often those that choose to live and feed in the large lakes where food is more abundant. For some reason real Alaska—not the part that lies adjacent to British Columbia—has few rivers boasting good stocks of anadromous rainbow trout AKA "steelheads". The closest thing is those rainbows migrating into the lakes to feed on baitfish there. They grow quite rapidly—a lot faster than would be possible in the rivers.

This particular rainbow trout was gorging itself on surplus salmon roe in a remote part of the Iliamna, Alaska area. It was lurking behind a bunch of spawning bright red sockeye salmon when it encountered my fluorescent Skykomish Sunrise fly—which it probably mistook for a blob of salmon roe.

In its first crazy run it jumped close to 20 times, thereby exhausting itself to such an extent that it only managed one more run before being beached. I didn't count the jumps myself as I was too busy keeping up with the running and jumping rainbow. My fishing companion did!

This particular fish was caught by a very young angler on his first (but not last) mission to Alaska. It weighed 9 pounds and made him come back for more!

Rainbow trout—Iliamna Lake—Alaska

REDFISH—
TEXAS

During the Second World War US naval personel listening for enemy submarines heard something strange. It took them quite a while to figure out what it was. And they were quite surprised to find that the noises came from redfish using their swimbladder as a drum when communicating!

Redfish are members of the drumfish family which lives in the warm western Atlantic and the Gulf of Mexico. They are highly specialized fish that grow up in very shallow water—the muddy flats of the Mexican Gulf. Here they spend most of their juvenile lives, migrating into deeper water as they grow bigger.

Redfish have that amiable look which you can only like. They simply look friendly though it is questionable if the shrimp and crabs of the same flats agree . . . And redfish swim flats flatter than any boat can ever float!

This means that you need specialized boats to get there. Boats that will float in very skinny water. Boats that are capable of rising out of this water when you turn the throttle. And boats so comfortable that it feels like you are fishing out of your favourite recliner!

Joking aside, Texan redfish are definitely worth a cast. But be prepared for a sudden tornado forcing you back to the harbor prematurely. This was what happened to us after experiencing some fantastic flyfishing for redfish in 6-8 inches of water. We barely made it. Sky turned from bright and sunny to pitch black in a few minutes. But fish hit like crazy until the storm was over us.

This particular redfish was taken on a small popper fly near Corpus Christi. The fish were stacked in shallow water where shrimp were migrating. In fact the water was so shallow that only poppers could be fished effectively.

The feeding redfish had to roll on their sides to engulf the floating flies with their typical overshot mouths. Quite a sight!

Redfish—Corpus Christi—Texas

RED ROCKFISH— GREENLAND

Rarely do you catch fish with pretty blue eyes. Fish that make you feel guilty when you think of actually killing and eating them. Fish that look accusingly at you with their big blue innocent eyes almost asking:—How could you?

Well, red rockfish are like that. Beautiful bright red fish with big blue eyes. They love really deep water but when you catch them there, they do not look their best—at least not when you bring them to the boat.

The sudden pressure difference has caused their pretty eyes to bulge out and their inflated swim bladder to force its way out of the mouth. But if you know where to catch them in shallow water, they look gorgeous.

I have a few favourite spots for catching red rockfish in Greenland. The hottest spot is also the prettiest. Here you bring your boat as close to the towering cliffs as possible until finally you are below a small waterfall coming off the top of the mountain. This is a setting so spectacular that you almost forget the fishing!

You will be fishing in water maybe 50 metres deep. And you will be fishing several hooks above your main lure. Red rockfish aren't big—seldom bigger than 1 kg—so you don't need heavy tackle. Also, you should not start winding in when you feel the first tug. Instead you wait a while for the rig to fill up with more redfish. Then you reel them all in!

Red rockfish are some of the tastiest fish to be found anywhere. Unfortunately, their numerous and very sharp spines make cleaning and filleting redfish a somewhat tricky affair. Unless you wear protective gloves.

Fortunately, their spines are not poisonous!

Red rockfish—Nuuk—Greenland

ROBALO—
TIERRA DEL FUEGO

When you travel half way across the globe to fish a remote area like Tierra del Fuego in South America, it is easy also to bring along your tunnel vision. Naturally, you are so focused on catching the particular fish you set out for, that you hardly notice other local fish species worth casting a fly to.

This is what almost happened to me. I was so intent on catching silvery sea trout fresh from the South Atlantic Ocean surrounding the island of Tierra del Fuego that it took me a while to appreciate the presence of another interesting game fish—the robalo.

It is a fish that roams the estuaries looking for migrating sea trout smolt on their way out into the ocean. A fish that thrives in brackish water and one of the very few indigenous fishes that actually thrive on the imported trout. Add to this that robalo have very tasty white meat and you will understand why the locals prefer them to trout!

After catching a few robalo and being impressed with their stubborn strength I started fishing for them specifically, leaving the sea trout behind for at least a while. My best results came using white Wooly Buggers that seemed very visible in the somewhat muddy water at high tide.

My dedicated robalo fishing resulted in some spectacular battles with these indigenous and hard fighting fish who do their very best to decimate the intruding sea trout. Trout seem to have completely taken over the South American rivers after their introduction some hundred years ago.

—Maybe it's finally payback time?

Robalo—Tierra del Fuego—Argentina

ROOSTERFISH— MEXICO

Catching a roosterfish on a fly is not for everyone. You need to be in the right place at the right time—and then have a little luck!

Roosterfish aren't very big but they are very pretty and pretty strong. Certainly they are fish with an attitude. Big roosterfish often hang out in the surf or in the breaking waves around offshore reefs and cliffs. This makes for some spectacular fishing where you often see the fish hunting in the waves and chasing your flies. Not for the faint of heart!

This particular roosterfish took an epoxy fly cast along a sandy beach on Mexico's Baja Peninsula. The fight was stubborn and the fish a trophy—my first rooster ever. It was released to fight another time—despite my Mexican guide's request that we bring it home and eat it.

What a beautiful fish with its rooster-like dorsal fin and wave-patterned back. Nature at its very best.

The Sea of Cortez had produced yet another unforgettable experience!

Roosterfish—Cabo San Lucas—Mexico

SARATOGA— AUSTRALIA

Saratoga are overlooked by the majority of fishermen going to Northern Australia in pursuit of the famed barramundi. But they are eagerly sought by the select few that know about them and have come to appreciate their affinity for surface feeding.

Saratoga are ancient looking fish with bony mouths that are very hard to set a hook into. Thus you will loose a lot of fish after striking them but that is the name of this game. Sometimes you win—most often you loose!

On the plus side is the fact that you hardly need open water to fish for this species. They prefer to hang out in areas of shallow water where the surface is covered with lily pads and similar water plants. Typically in "billabongs"—the sweet Aussie name for river bends cut off from the main river.

To get in on the action—without getting hung up on every single cast—you need weedless flies that may crawl across the lily pads, just waiting to be picked up by eager bonymouths in the tiny pieces of open water.

Once hooked saratoga put up a great fight with lots of aerobatics. Chaos is probably the word best describing this particular kind of semi-dry Aussie fishing . . .

Billabong fishing at its best!

Saratoga—Northern Territory—Australia

SEA BASS—
IRELAND

Seabass are to British fishermen what seatrout are to Danish—the game fish numero uno!

It is a species native to the British Channel and surrounding countries. One of the most important game fishes on both sides of the channel—in Ireland, England, France and Holland. Everywhere it is found, it is highly sought after—unfortunately not only by sport fishermen. Commercial fishermen also target it increasingly, putting a lot of pressure on diminishing fish stocks.

At the same time it is a species on its way north with the ever increasing ocean temperatures. As is the case with mullet, anchovies and other warm water fish species. They all migrate north as the ocean warms. At the same time cold water species like cod move even further north—towards colder water. They feel the threat from the warmer waters that don't allow their offspring to thrive.

Today, good numbers of seabass are caught from Danish and Norwegian shorelines—primarily from May through October where water temperatures are suitable for this fish. They present an entirely new way of fishing as they require different tactics and different tackle.

This particular specimen was caught in the strong tidal curents along the southeastern Irish coast. Next stop here is France!

Sea bass—Bannow Bay—Ireland

SEA TROUT—
ARGENTINA

It is a strange fact that some of the world's best seatrout fishing is to be had in Tierra del Fuego—the southernmost tip of South America.

Strange as no trout or salmon are indigenous to the southern hemisphere. Instead they have been planted here by man—by the flyfishing British colonialists—and they have thrived beyond all expectations. The cold but fertile waters of the southern Atlantic Ocean teem with food and thus make for some of the world's largest seatrout.

Probably the world's most famous and productive seatrout river is the Rio Grande. It originates in the Chilean part of Tierra del Fuego and winds its way down towards the Argentinean part where it meets the ocean.

It is often and jokingly called "Old Man River"—not to be mistaken for the mighty Mississippi—as its flat and sandy bottom makes for very easy wading. Even if you happen to be an elderly gentleman with high hopes of catching the seatrout of a lifetime. Flying down to Rio Grande it is difficult *not* to notice the high average age of the passengers!

This particular seatrout was caught in the tidal pool where the river meets the ocean. Wading the muddy bottom here is not for the faint of heart. Ever so often you get stuck in the mud—faced with a potentially fatal tidal difference of several metres . . .

And then there is the ever blowing wind. Flyfishing in Tierra del Fuego has been likened to fishing in a wind tunnel.

I am not one to disagree . . .

Sea trout—Tierra del Fuego—Argentina

SEA TROUT—
DENMARK

Tiny Denmark undoubtedly boasts some of the most prolific seatrout fishing in the whole wide world. Despite its small size Denmark offers some 7.500 km of productive shallow coastline teeming with food items like baitfish, shrimps and lugworms—all resulting in quick growth of seatrout during their saltwater stay.

Season is all year long with spring and autumn being the most productive. Seatrout migrate a lot—governed by salinity and temperature—so to be successful you have to follow them wherever they go.

Most fishing is done walking the shoreline or wading the beaches. But a float tube, pontoon boat or a regular boat can be very helpful in locating the fish and getting from one place to another.

Originally, Danish seatrout fishing was done exclusively by spinning. Today the pendulum has swung in favor of flyfishing which has become increasingly and in many places incredibly popular. Thousands of Danish flyfishermen probe the salty flats and weed beds every day of the year, catching thousands of salty silvery seatrout.

This particular seatrout was caught off the coast of Samsoe island where annual seatrout flyfishing courses have been held for the last 11 years—all fully booked.

Quite a few of the participants have come from outside of tiny Denmark so our reputation must have spread and gone international!

Sea trout—Samsø Island—Denmark

SEA TROUT II— DENMARK

The island of *Bornholm* is the easternmost part of the Danish kingdom. It boasts cliffs that the rest of Denmark doesn't. Here sandy and pebbly beaches dominate.

Bornholm is also home to numerous seatrout being spawned in the many small burns that criss-cross the rocky island. The mature seatrout offer great shoreline fishing for both fly and spin fishermen.

Lately, Bornholm has gained international fame for its offshore salmon fishing in the deep Baltic Sea surrounding the island. Salmon come to the waters around Bornholm in the southern Baltic to feed on the plentiful sprat and herring found here.

Trolling is the way to catch these silvery 5-25 kg beauties in waters often reaching 50-100 metres. Trolling with downriggers and cannonballs.

Usually shoreline seatrout don't mingle with salmon that prefer deeper water. But there are exceptions. This particular seatrout was one such notable exception to this rule. It was caught in deep water but relatively close to the rocky shore.

10 pounds of silvery seatrout glistening in the hot sun of June!

Sea trout—Bornholm—Denmark

SEA TROUT—
NORWAY

For seatrout the night time is definitely the right time.

Seatrout are nocturnal fish—especially so in freshwater where they like to hug banks and hide in the deep or behind underwater roots during daytime. When darkness comes, they become active and seek the shallows. Here they are vulnerable to a big black silhuette fly fished on a floating line.

Fishing in a pitch black, maybe rainy and sometimes bitterly cold Scandinavian night is not for everybody. You have to be in full command of your tackle which you cannot see. You have to feel and listen your way through the night!

If that is not the case with you, you shouldn't even try. Instead you should opt for daytime salmon fishing. Luckily, seatrout and salmon match each other perfectly. Salmon are active in daylight—seatrout during the night. The choice is yours!

This particular seatrout was caught around midnight in a shallow Norwegian river together with a handful of its smaller brethren—silvery and fresh run fish weighing up to 4 pounds.

The big one pictured here weighed close to 12 pounds, struck a small black fly very close to shore and was beached only some fifty yards downstream of where it took the fly.

It certainly made my day—sorry, night!

Sea trout—Jølstra River—Norway

SILVER SALMON—
ALASKA

Sometimes you just need to catch fish—large ones and plenty of them. You may simply need to boost your ego after some fishless outings . . .

Well, if that is the problem, I have the solution:—Go silver salmon fishing in Alaska! If you hit it right, you will catch loads of strong silvery beauties fresh from the Pacific. Your rod will bend deep and your reel will be screaming out loud. Just what any fisherman needs . . .

I once treated myself to this, by visiting the beautiful Tsiu River in September. I was walking in the footsteps of famous Danish explorer Vitus Bering who, during the early part of the 18th century, explored and discovered this part of the world for the Russian Tzar. That was before the Russians sold Alaska to the Americans!

Unfortunately, Bering died while exploring Alaska and was buried here, the place of his death later given his name. He stranded here with his men, ran out of food and into scurvy—and subsequently died in the freezing cold of the Alaskan winter.

As a travelling Dane I am naturally proud to know that one of my fellow Danes has given name to both the Bering Glacier, the Bering Island and the Bering Sea. Quite an accomplishment.

But back to the Tsiu River. Let me tell you, without lying the least, that in one week I caught way over 100 bright silver salmon, all fresh from the Pacific. They all took a silvery Xmas Tree fly, they all weighed between 4 and 7 kg's, and they all put up a great fight before giving up and letting me beach them gently—before releasing them back into the river again.

Thus I returned to Denmark with a boosted ego and a fully restored self confidence.

Just what the doctor ordered . . . !

Silver salmon—Tsiu River—Alaska

SMALLSPOTTED DART— MALDIVES

They don't have to be big to be beautiful. The old saying was proven by the small spotted darts that took my tiny fly while I was wading a beautiful sandy flat in the magnificent Maldives. These fish are just so pretty!

And the darts certainly were not shy. In fact small schools of them were finning around our legs all the time while we were wading or swimming in the turquoise waters found here. A scenery completely out of this world—which it may soon be if we let climate change, global warming and rising oceans swallow these sandy beauties. It hurts just to think of it . . .

When not walking the beaches or wading the flats we were snorkeling the amazing coral reefs surrounding the Maldives. If you have never done that before, it is high time to go!

Out here you will encounter basking sea turtles, black—and whitetipped reef sharks finning around in the deep cobolblue water, bluespotted rays lying on the white sandy bottom, aggressive triggerfish protecting their terrritory and a whole host of other colorful reef fish species.

The world above water will never be the same again . . .

Sample the Maldives—now!

Smallspotted dart—Merufenfushi—Maldives

SOCKEYE SALMON—
ALASKA

Pacific salmon are among the most amazing fish in the whole wide world. If for no other reason than the fact that they literally sacrifice their own lives for the sake of their offspring. Having finished spawning, all Pacific salmon die. And I mean all. In fact you could say that mortality is 110%!

Whereas some Atlantic salmon survive spawning, all Pacific ones die. There is much speculation behind this strange phenomenon but it is generally agreed that in doing so the parent fish fertilize the often sterile waters so that they may provide more food for their own offspring.

It has also been calculated that in areas of temperate rain forests, Pacific salmon contribute up to 80% of all nitrogen to the ecosystem on land. Meaning that there would be very few trees had it not been for the Pacific salmon which pick up the necessary nitrogen while feeding in the rich open ocean and bring it back inland. Well worth some consideration when discussing the wise management of endangered salmon stocks . . .

The sockeye salmon pictured here is probably the most specialized of the five species of Pacific salmon inhabiting North America. It is born in or near lakes where the juveniles grow up. Out in the Pacific the young sockeyes feed on crustaceans almost exclusively, giving them their highly treasured bright red flesh. The only salmon flesh that stays red after cooking and canning.

Years ago it was an accepted fact that you simply could not catch sockeye salmon on hook and line. They just did not respond. But then it was discovered that you can often lure them into taking small flies that probably remind them of their ocean feeding.

Only rarely do sockeye salmon strike lures. They simply don't know what to do with them!

Sockeye salmon—Iliamna Lake—Alaska

SPOTTED WOLFFISH— GREENLAND

Greenland is an amazing place to be—fantastic for fishing too. Most fishermen go there for arctic char which are found almost everywhere but a few hardy fishermen will target halibut specifically.

They will not catch a lot of fish as halibut are rare but they will get good numbers of large wolffish while searching for the giant flounders. Quite often these spotted monsters will exceed 40 pounds.

And they will hiss alarmingly at you when they surface. Water and air squeezed through their narrow gill slits make them sound pretty scary. But then again—it may or may not be personal!

If you want to keep one for eating—and they are pretty tasty—it is very advisable to first finish them off with a .22 rifle! Their big rounded teeth and incredibly strong jaws will crunch anything that gets in there. So do keep your precious fingers out . . .

In them good old days the skin of spotted wolffish was tanned and used for making shoes. It is that tough!

Spotted wolffish—Nuuk—Greenland

STEELHEAD—
BRITISH COLUMBIA

—Son, if you want to catch a really big steelhead—go north!

That was the advice given to me by an oldtime steelheader in Washington way back in the good old 1980's.

I followed his advice and ended up on the banks of the remote Sustut River in northern British Columbia. A helicopter was the only way of getting in as weather was bad and cloud cover low.

But it was well worth it. I ended up catching five steelhead that week, weighing from 15 to 20 pounds each. All on flies and single handed rods. The more miserable the weather, the better the fishing! Every night we returned to the lodge with numb fingers and icy knees. Remember, this was in the days before neoprene waders and fleece pants . . .

On the last morning, just before departure, I was debating with myself whether to enjoy a hot and steaming cup of coffee—or go fishing one last time. Ice was covering the floor boards of our river boat and it was bitterly cold. Freshly fallen snow was covering the mountains.

Contemplating my own sanity, I donned my icy PVC waders, grabbed my 10 foot fly rod and made a few casts. Just as the helicopter showed above the trees, a beautiful 15 pounder took my Xmas Tree fly and put up a good show for the pilot!

I didn't make another cast. It would have ruined the whole experience. It always pays to stop when you have reached the top!

Also, it was time to climb into the helicopter and go back to Denmark.

Mission accomplished!

Steelhead—Sustut River—British Columbia

STEELHEAD— OREGON

Steelhead are to westcoast anglers what Atlantic salmon are to eastcoast fishermen—the most sought after game fish. From a fishing point of view, they behave pretty much the same.

Steelhead are anadromous rainbow trout that migrate from their rivers of birth to feed and grow in the Pacific—just like the Pacific salmon do. Heavy feeding makes them grow big with 20 pounds being the magical limit for steelhead anglers. And 30 pounders do exist!

Most steelhead are much smaller—especially in the lower US. Washington and Oregon are strongholds for this magnificent fish which has been in for a hard time in California. Today the fishing typically gets better the further north you go—with nothing much left of the original California steelhead.

Oregon still has plenty of great steelhead water—much of it located in the desert where you will be fishing in the company of skunks and rattlesnakes! That knowledge certainly adds to the excitement when you have to climb the banks to claim the fly that was caught on your back cast—in the dense sage brush.

Luckily, most rattlesnakes will let you know when you get too close. Just listen. And the awful smell of a nearby skunk leaves nobody in doubt. Even when you drive by one on the road, you can smell it!

The steelhead pictured here was caught in one of the many small rivers in Oregon bearing the name "Salmon River".

It was my first steelhead ever and it left a lasting impression.

Plus it put a silly smile on my face!

Steelhead—Salmon River—Oregon

STRIPED BASS—
NEW HAMPSHIRE

Striped bass are popular game fish in Northeast America. One of the most sought after.

They migrate up and down the eastcoast, maybe spawning down south in the Chesapeake Bay and getting caught up north, off the shores of Martha's Vineyard. Everywhere found they are greeted by eager fisherman wanting both their fierce fight and their tasty meat.

The latter was reason enough for once bringing this great fish on the brink of extinction. Heavy netting took its toll, and bass populations couldn't support themselves any longer. Finally and luckily, national authorities solved the problem by imposing severe restrictions on commercial fishing.

Success was immediate and recovery of stocks impressive. Today striped bass provide both sport and income to anglers and fishing guides in many eastcoast states. Angling tourism now accounts for way more income and tax money than commercial netting ever did.

Being true migratory fish, striped bass thrive in both fresh and salt water. This particular bass was caught in the Merrimack River in New Hampshire and took a Clouser Minnow just subsurface.

Fishing took place in the early, early morning—at sunrise.

And I hate mornings . . .

Striped bass—Merrimack River—New Hampshire

SURUBI—
PERU

The mighty Amazon River is host to a multitude of different fish species. In fact several thousands of them.

Amongst them are quite a few catfish that thrive in the dark and often muddy water found here. They rely more on their acute sense of smell than on their often poor eyesight.

If you are lucky, you will hook up with a giant surubi or tiger catfish as they are also called. You cannot mistake it for anything else—due to its marked tiger stripes and dark spots. Also, the surubi is the largest catfish that you will likely encounter here, bigger specimens often exceeding 10 kg's with the odd one crossing the 20 kg mark.

The surubi is known to grow larger than 50 kg's—if allowed to. But since it has very tasty meat, it is highly sought after by the locals who fish stocks hard. Monofilament nets are the preferred way of catching surubi. And very efficient in the murky waters of the Amazon.

Surubis are aggressive catfish that—unlike their bottom dwelling relatives—often strike surface lures cast for other species.

As you can see from this picture, surubis are fish with plenty of personality and loads of attitude!

Surubi—Amazon River—Peru

TAIMEN—
SIBERIA

Taimen are members of the ancient Hucho genus and by many believed to be the forefathers of all modern salmonoids.

And sure enough: If you take a close look at a big taimen or even better, the smaller lenok, they seem to have all the traits found in both salmon, trout, char and grayling. Thus it is easy to understand why this hypothesis has arised.

Anyway, from a sportfishing point of view taimen are of particular interest—simply because they are believed to be the largest member of the salmonid fishes. Fish in excess of 50 kg have been caught and bigger ones are believed or rumoured to exist or have existed.

Taimen feed heavily on anything that moves. In Siberia its daily diet of baitfish is heavily supplemented by eating rodents—mice, lemmings and even squirrels—that acidentally fall into the water or go for a swim to cross a river. The mighty taimen stuns his prey with a splash of his giant tail. After that it is easy business picking up the stunned animals . . .

This particular taimen was relatively small—less than 30 pounds—and was caught spinning. We were on a rough two week rafting trip in the Yakutsk area and had only what we caught on our way to eat. Subsequently we had fish for breakfast, supper and dinner . . .

So this taimen was not released to fight again but greedily devoured by us and our Russian guides.

When in Siberia, you have to eat what you catch.

Or go to bed hungry . . .

Taimen—Lena River—Sibiria

TARPON—
COSTA RICA

Tarpon are among the most sought after game fish in the world. And for a very good reason. No other fish jumps as much and as high as do tarpon!

Add to this the fact that tarpon grow BIG. Catching a 100 pound+ tarpon is nothing unusual—even on a fly rod! But you will hook and jump a lot more tarpon than you actually land. Tarpon are masters of throwing hooks that do not get a good hold in their toothless but very bony mouths.

Tarpon are ancient-looking, herring-like creatures that can actually breathe air in addition to extracting oxygen from the water. They may gulp air when the water is low on oxygen. This means that they are very surface-orientated, often seen rolling as they move along. "Sabalo banjo" as the locals say in Spanish. Rolling tarpon.

This also means that tarpon are vulnerable to flies presented on or just below the surface. In this respect it is an additional help to the flyfisherman that tarpon—despite their often impressive size—primarily rely on small baitfish and crustaceans for food. Thus tarpon are a flyfisherman's dream fish.

In Florida you sight fish for tarpon, casting only to tarpon that you have seen. In Costa Rica you do a lot of blind fishing but occasionally have a shot at moving tarpon. The rolling fish reveal themselves through a string of trailing bubbles on the surface. Here you have to cast a sinking fly on a sinking line, well ahead of the bubbles. An then wait for the ever so subtle take . . .

This particular tarpon was caught at the mouth of the Rio Colorado in Costa Rica. On a fairly small #1/0 red-and-white Whistler fly.

Tarpon—Rio Colorado—Costa Rica

TENCH—
DENMARK

Some fish just have more personality than others. Some are aggressive, some are peaceful, and some are just plain pretty. And then you have the wise ones—at least the fish species that *look* wise!

Tench are definitely members of the wise-looking fish group. They are also pretty good-looking. Add to this their longstanding reputation of being the "doctor" among freshwater fishes. Their ruby red eyes, large and velvety fins plus their thick slime coating is what gives them that wise look always associated with doctors.

Thus the story goes that the sick fishes of a lake will seek the healing company of the wise tench. Even the father of all modern sportfishing, Izaak Walton from good old England, knew that to be true. So who are we to doubt?

From a fisherman's point of view, tench may indeed behave wisely. At least they can be very good at avoiding a hook embedded in even the most delicious bait—be it corn from the can, a lively maggot or better yet: A wriggling earth worm.

Just like their close relative, the common carp, tench seem to have that sixth sense which tells them if and when something is terribly wrong. And when that happens, you can kiss your tench goodbye!

They also have incredibly good hearing made possible by specialized bones linking their inner ear to their swim bladder. The latter then acts as an amplifier of surrounding sounds.

So when you go tench fishing, move slowly and make no noise. Soundwaves travel far under water . . .

Tench—Nørresø—Denmark

TIGERFISH—
NAMIBIA

There is something absolutely terrifying about African tigerfish. They live in some beautiful albeit merciless and unforgiving territory. They have razorsharp triangular teeth that will cut anything in two—except the best of single strand steel wire traces.

And they strike visciously—as no other fish on earth—when they are in that mood. If you hook them in a strong Zambezi River current, there is just no stopping them. Or keeping them from jumping and possibly throwing that hook . . .

On the other hand, there are times when these top predators can be very shy and difficult to tease into striking. Especially if the water temperature suddenly drops. Their viscious strikes will then be mere nibbles into the feathers of your flies. Making them very hard to hook.

This particular specimen weighed in at 15 pounds plus and struck a #1 Xmas Tree fly in a dark Namibian night. We were later chased away from the spot by an angry bull hippo that really scared the hell out of my white guide. Most probably he knew better than me how dangerous the situation was.

Statistically, more Africans are killed by angry and territorial hippos than by any other animals. Lions, hyenas, crocodiles and snakes included . . . Hippos may look docile and peaceful—but they definitely aren't!

Judging from the available journals, the tigerfish pictured was the second largest tigerfish ever caught on fly in the Zambezi River system. And an IGFA world record if I had cared to register it. Which I didn't do.

But it was certainly one of my best experiences ever!

Tigerfish—Zambezi River—Namibia

TRIGGERFISH—
MALDIVES

Titan triggerfish are not normally caught on rod and line, being the convinced coral crunchers that they are.

Triggerfish are also very aggressive, defending their territories vigorously against intruders—be they divers a hundred times bigger than themselves. They will chase you around and bite your swim fins!

Scientists believe that triggerfish are responsible for producing up to maybe one third of all coral sand found—simply by crushing corals and passing them through their stomachs! They are certainly helped by other coral munching and crunching species like parrotfish.

This estimate may or may not be true. Fact remains that they do crush a lot of corals when they feed. Any diver can experience this himself by approaching a feeding triggerfish. Their munching and crunching can be clearly heard under water!

Their feeding behaviour puts triggerfish out of range of most sportfishing methods. This particular Titan Triggerfish from beautiful Maldives was the exception to the rule.

It jumped on a red plastic jig which didn't live to tell about it. It was crunched beyond recognition . . .

Titan triggerfish—Merufenfushi—Maldives

WAHOO—
MALDIVES

Nobel Prize winning author and fisherman Ernest Hemingway was once asked what fish he ranked number one for eating.

He didn't hesitate to declare that wahoo are the best eating, fastest running and hardest fighting fish in the ocean! And Hemingway should know as he had been battling marlin and tuna many times bigger than wahoo.

Well, taste is a personal thing but fact is that wahoo are among the fastest swimming creatures in the ocean. Long, slim and extremely fast, these streamlined beauties put up a tremendous fight when hooked and played on light tackle.

Usually wahoo are too quick for flyfishing. You simply cannot strip that fly fast enough through the water to attract their attention. They don't recognize anything that slow as potential food!

This particular wahoo was caught trolling off the coast of the beautiful Maldives which are in danger of disappearing completely from the Earth's surface—due to climate change, increasing water temperatures and rising ocean levels.

What a shame—and shame on us for bringing it so far . . .

I get sad whenever I think of it.

Wahoo—Merufenfushi—Maldives

YELLOWTAIL SNAPPER— CUBA

Ever so often you run into fish species that you did not know about or had never seen before. Fish so striking that you never doubted their ability to recognize colours. Why would they have these bright colours if they couldn't see them?

And they can. Scientists know that almost all of the 30.000 species of bony fishes—*Osteichtyes* between fish scientists—have a very well developed ability to recognize and distinguish colours. They also know that sharks and rays have a very limited colour vision—if any at all.

But bony fishes are easily as good at colours as we humans are—with an inclination towards being even better at recognizing colours in the blue end of the spectrum. This is not surprising as blue is the dominant colour in deeper water, with red being the first colour to be absorbed and disappear underwater.

This particular yellowtail snapper was caught on a small upside down Xmas Tree fly while fishing for bonefish in the Jardines de la Reina national park in Cuba.

I just couldn't help taking its picture!

Yellowtail snapper—Jardines de la Reina—Cuba

ZANDER—
DENMARK

Zander or pikeperch are particular fish with peculiar habits. Though you may catch them during the day, the night time definitely is the right time for zander fishing.

Their glassy eyes are specifically adapted to low light hunting as they have an extra layer designed to reflect and amplify the available light. Still zander are slow fish that need a lot of time to make up their minds. Slow trolling with rattling wobblers or live bait fishing is thus the preferred method for catching this interesting and most delicious fish.

Only occasionaly can you catch them on flies. But it certainly can be done as I have proved on several occasions. Best time for this is just before and right after spawning which takes place in late spring in shallow water over a rocky bottom. Here zander will even be active during daytime. And here you may well catch them on flies in the brightest of sunshine!

The pictured specimen weighed in at 13 pounds and is my best ever zander. It was caught around midnight on a bitterly cold night in March. When the sun set, the cold crept in. And when we returned to shore, a thin layer of ice had formed over the boat. Brrrr . . .

My best ever zander was released to spawn another time. It feels pretty good to know that in all probability it is still out there in the dark!

Zander—River Guden—Denmark

ONE MORE THING . . .

A book like this is a never ending story. The quest goes on, and new species are constantly—at least hopefully!—added to the list. Thus the book will keep growing for years to come.

Browsing through its electronic pages you will come across a fly called the "Xmas Tree"—shown on page 73. Here in Denmark it is well known and widely used—especially for seatrout fishing in the salt. But it will catch all kinds of species—all over the world. You just have to tie it differently—long or short, upside down etc. It is very adaptable and I never leave home without it!

It is my baby and I am proud of it! Here's how a basic Xmas Tree is tied:

Hook: Mustad 34007 # 1-8
Thread: fluorescent red nylon
Underbody: fluorescent red chenille
Tail: pearl mylar tubing
Body: pearl mylar tubing
Hackle: pearl mylar tubing

It can be tied in all thinkable and available colours but only a handful have proven worthy of mentioning: The original *pearl*—suitable and productive under all conditions. *Fluorescent red*—perfect for cold water and overcast days. *Fluorescent green*—ideal for nighttime fishing as it can be charged with a flashlight. And finally plain *silver*—great for the largest hooks. Enjoy!

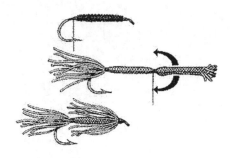

Steen Ulnits

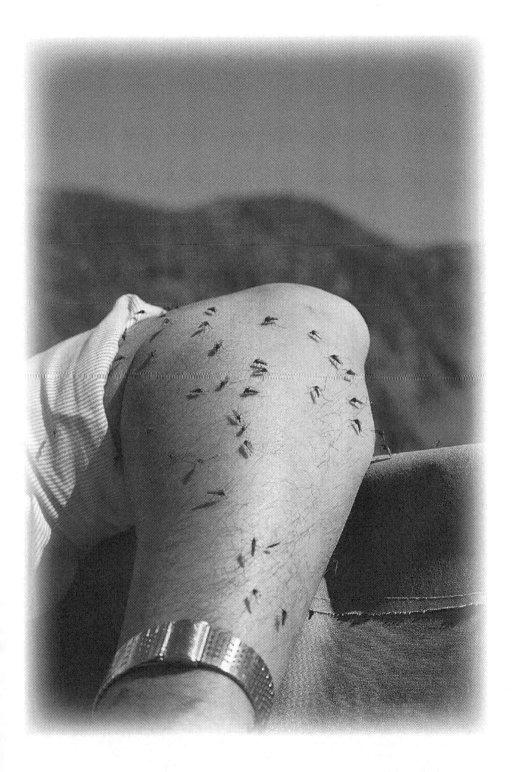